FEATHERED FRIENDS

ROBINS

Kim Thompson

NORWOOD HOUSE PRESS

Cataloging-in-Publication Data

Names: Thompson, Kim.
Title: Robins / Kim Thompson.
Description: Buffalo, NY : Norwood House Press, 2027. | Series: Feathered friends | Includes glossary and index.
Identifiers: ISBN 9781978580534 (pbk.) | ISBN 9781978580541 (library bound) | ISBN 9781978580558 (ebook)
Subjects: LCSH: Robins--Juvenile literature. | Robins--Life cycles--Juvenile literature.
Classification: LCC QL696.P288 T548 2027 | DDC 598.842--dc23

Published in 2027 by
Norwood House Press
2544 Clinton Street
Buffalo, NY 14224

Designer: Rhea Magaro
Editor: Tricia Hoffman

Photo credits: Cover, p.1 Bachkova Natalia/Shutterstock.com; p.5 Wirestock Creators/Shutterstock.com; p.6 Larry Burk/Shutterstock.com; p.7 Lee O'Dwyer/Shutterstock.com; p.9 Tracy Morris/Shutterstock.com; p.10 Max Forgues/Shutterstock.com; p.13 shaftinaction/Shutterstock.com; p.14 Wirestock Creators/Shutterstock.com; p.17 kstuart/Shutterstock.com; p.18 Tony Quinn/Shutterstock.com; p.21 Craig Sterken/Shutterstock.com;

Printed in the United States of America

TABLE OF CONTENTS

What Do Robins Look Like?

Robins are our feathered friends. You can recognize them by their reddish-orange chests. They have pointy yellow **beaks** and dark heads. Their eyes are outlined in white.

Compared to many songbirds, robins are big. They have long legs and plump bodies. They are about as long as two stacked soda cans.

A robin's long tail helps it balance.

Where Do Robins Live?

American robins live across Canada and the United States and in parts of Mexico. In winter, many **migrate** from north to south to find food. People look for the returning robins as a sign of spring.

Robins are not picky about where they live. You can find them in yards, parks, fields, and forests.

How Do Robins Grow Up?

During the spring and summer, robins lay eggs two or three times. Each time, the female lays a **clutch** of about four blue eggs.

Babies **hatch** in two weeks. After about a month, they can fly.

What Do Robins Eat?

Beginning early in the morning, robins hop in the grass looking for worms. When they find one, they use their beaks to tug it from the dirt and gobble it up. Have you ever heard the old saying "the early bird gets the worm"? It is about a robin!

Besides worms, robins also eat insects such as caterpillars and grasshoppers.

In fall and winter, they look for fruits and berries.

What Sounds Do Robins Make?

Robins are known for their **cheerful** singing. In spring and summer, their calls are some of the earliest morning sounds. They begin singing before **dawn**. They also sing at **dusk**.

Male robins sing to protect their **territories** and to find females. Their calls sound like this: "cheer-up, cheerily, cheer-up, cheerily."

What Funny Things Can Robins Do?

Robins know that it is easier to find worms in wet soil. After it rains, or after playing in the sprinkler, look for robins bopping along to find their favorite meal.

GLOSSARY

beaks (beeks): horny, pointed jaws on birds; bird bills

cheerful (CHEER-fuhl): full of happiness

clutch (kluhch): all the eggs laid in a nest at the same time

dawn (dawn): the time of day when the sun rises and it starts to get light

dusk (duhsk): the time of day after sunset when it starts to get dark

hatch (hach): to break out of an egg to be born

migrate (MYE-grate): to move from one area or climate to another at a certain time of the year

territories (TER-i-tor-eez): areas that are defended by an animal and that often contain the animal's home

THINKING QUESTIONS

1. Why do people think of robins as a sign of spring?

2. Where do robins live?

3. About how many eggs do robins lay each year?

4. Why do robins hop in the grass?

5. What does a male robin's song sound like?

INDEX

ABOUT THE AUTHOR

Kim Thompson is a writer from Columbus, Ohio. She has written many books for kids. Lots of birds come to her backyard feeder. Her favorites are the showy red cardinals, tiny bright goldfinches, and waddling mallard ducks. Her two cats watch from the window.